DUNK TANK

Also by Kayla Czaga

For Your Safety Please Hold On

DUNK TANK

KAYLA CZAGA

ANANSI

Published in Canada in 2019 and the USA in 2019 by House of Anansi Press Inc.
www.houseofanansi.com

23 22 21 20 19   1 2 3 4 5

Library and Archives Canada Cataloguing in Publication

Czaga, Kayla, author
Dunk tank / Kayla Czaga.

Poems.
Issued in print and electronic formats.
ISBN 978-1-4870-0596-2 (softcover).—ISBN 978-1-4870-0597-9 (hardcover).—
ISBN 978-1-4870-0598-6 (PDF)

I. Title.

PS8605.Z34D86 2019   C811'.6   C2018-904722-4
                          C2018-904723-2

Library of Congress Control Number: 2018958297

Book design: Alysia Shewchuk

Canada Council   Conseil des Arts
for the Arts   du Canada

ONTARIO ARTS COUNCIL
CONSEIL DES ARTS DE L'ONTARIO
an Ontario government agency
un organisme du gouvernement de l'Ontario

We acknowledge for their financial support of our publishing program the Canada Council for the Arts, the Ontario Arts Council, and the Government of Canada.

Printed and bound in Canada

CONTENTS

I

II

III

IV

I

The girl with mercurial eyes reads minds, solves
crimes, and finds a solid-eyed boy to love.

The angry boy who sleeps under
his uncle's staircase whispers to snakes.

Loved by sad girls everywhere the suicide poet
is immortalized. The siblings with six toes

hike to utopia. You ate a cloud and felt
cold for sixteen years. You ate the ghost
of Sylvia Plath all afternoon

in your lilac room and tried to identify
the defect that will qualify you
as a heroine. You touch your navel

twenty times, but no Narnia appears.
In dreams sometimes you fly
but mostly loiter the mall and skip

over lava in Bowser's castle.
Could living in Alaska's armpit be your defect,
your town so small it's been allotted no

dot on the map? From where you're
standing the world is four liquor stores

and an aluminum smelter. It ends
at the treeline on Elizabeth Mountain.

The world is a series of streets named
after birds, which form a circle with no
beginning, every driveway a dead end.

THE MISTS OF AVALON

While the grade sevens shaded the chocolate
paws of grizzly bears, you—lowly third grader—
dotted frogs on the school's flora and fauna mural.
You could spell *veterinarian, library,* and *February,*
so detailing amphibians felt insultingly below
your skill level. You wept when you saw a Texan
kitten born with two faces on the dinnertime news.
The injustice of the world. *Teen Cosmo* called
you a "soft tomboy" because you liked nail polish
and entomology. *Seventeen* told you to repeat
jewel tones until people noticed the green specks
in your eyes, then surely your life would change.
Taking sad lyrics as life advice was among
your worst character flaws, as was wishing
your name was Guinevere. Another dust-purple
afternoon waiting, what for? On your dresser
snow globe water yellowed like May snow,
adult teeth, and your early report cards.
Smart girl, they said in every season. Then again,
you'd always thought if you waited long enough
you'd see popcorn kernels pop in the sun.

One Christmas, Santa gave you a set of panties
so jumbo you called them your thunderpants.
Wherever you went you went with thunderpants
in your navel. You loved the way they left deep
red runnels around your midriff, loved them
the way one loves an icky childhood teddy.
They made your butt look like a Greek column
of clouds, divined by the Delphic oracle
as an omen of great olive forbearance. Such
were the days you loved your butt in billowy
rainbow parachutes. You were seven and showed
off your thunderpants to grocery store strangers
every chance you got, believing your butt
would become a skydiver or even prime minister
of Canada. Who was he who made you—
so many years and underwear sets later, in that
Honda Civic's backseat—believe differently?

Fortunetellers, swans, love boats,
whole notebooks shredded over
whether Justin M kissed Kyra D
on Thursday and should we
invite Sally or Jenny to the lake?
You'd subtract the numbers by day
of the month, ages you wanted to be
married by, then convert them
through a secret handshake back
into letters. After walking home
you'd all phone each other despite
living two blocks apart and having
just spent seven hours synchronized
eye-rolling. Remember dyeing half
of Deandra's hair before the school
dance of never being asked to dance?
Oh, you were inept and sweaty
but everything was urgent enough
to be the season finale, every day,
every second in your volcanic skin.
No wonder you now fear every girl
that age. The way they love a girl
at recess, stringing dandelions
around her neck, then shed her
like last season's sweater, having
grown bored of her and everything.

FALSE NOON ON HIGHWAY 16

The black X on the calendar meant
your dad wasn't coming home,
would inhale aluminum filaments
at the smelter to finance your future.
Funny how he always had a better view
on your future than you did.
You could only see as far ahead
as Kristie's headlights tonguing
the dark along the highway to Smithers.
At the college party, you didn't
know lyrics to indie songs, laughed
at twice-told jokes. Girl, your Kitimat
showed. A moose head with bras
dangling off its antlers made you
hug your chest and curl in a corner
of the tongue-coloured couch.
You woke to Kristie pushing on
your boots, a clock blinking noon
though you knew it was lying.
She smelled like cigarettes and boy
deodorant, like a person you didn't
know. Her car coughed on.
Grey mist fingered the clouds,
rubbed against bushes. You wanted
to tell Kristie that the cow with legs
tucked under its body looked legless,
like someone'd lopped them off,
left it bobbing for dead in the field.
She didn't speak, kept checking
her rearview. *Stop here*—
you wanted to say, then grab her
hand and pull her towards the warm
animal in the field, to find its legs

together and prove to her that things
weren't always how they appeared.
You wanted to take her face and kiss
the apathy off it while her keys
dangled and engine exhausted itself.
Instead, you let her drop you at home,
crawled in your bedroom window.
By the time you'd shimmied inside
her car was gone. You watched her
headlights' glow fade like a feeling
you once believed was permanent.

DUNK TANK

The volleyball girls wrestle in Jell-O.
Travis Lechner, lead screamer
of Occult Nosebleed, commands
the tenth-grade stoners to *live real*.
The French teacher struts
like a heron, beige socks hiked up
to his knees. You've been suckered
into a shift at the dunk tank
to fundraise for a school in Tanzania.
You'll be dunked six times—
twice by a boy named Brice you love
but never talk to. When he runs out
of money, he'll throw grass
at you, chunks of hotdog, himself.
You climb up and wave
to your friends eating Filipino kebabs
by the track. Tonight you'll all
drink coolers by the waterfall.
This is the year Dustin Klepsch will drive
his ATV off a cliff. You sit
above the drunk goggle obstacle
course and rootbeer-guzzling contest
and you know you know everything—
can diagram reproductive systems
of worms, know exactly when
two trains travelling 60km/hour
will meet in Kitwanga for lunch.
This is the year your mom's kidneys
will fail while you're in History
and the year Kristie will stop talking
to you and painting sad-lovely
portraits of her dogs. Brice pays
two dollars to throw three balls

at you. The wind sighs like it's locked
its keys in its car. You're sitting
on your chair, smart girl, only
your chair drops and before you fall
there's this moment you're sitting
on nothing and you think maybe
you won't fall after all—maybe
you'll just hover here forever.

We could read your words from anywhere
but you felt like the only soul sitting
in your swivel chair listening to your parents

dream-breathing down the hall while you typed
to boys from Kelowna and Trinidad about
your boredom and body. You blogged

about the three-legged moose you saw
on the highway to Terrace, the lonely red
radio light on top of a mountain. A boy

from Michigan called you on the phone.
His voice reminded you of a TV show.
It was dawn there, Detroit already falling

like an ancient empire. In the photo he sent
his face was obscured by a trucker hat.
Was the internet a series of tubes, or something

scientists kept in a room in California?
Did a robot army of spiders weave its connections?
In every post, you were the lonely red radio light

we could see from the airport but never get close to.
You gave virtual blowjobs, saw how other
kids in other towns cut themselves, how other

kids walked around other ice rinks with other
problems and frenemies. After school
you lived different versions of the same.

What's your favourite colour? Sometimes yellow,
mostly red. *Who's your best friend?*
What's the one thing you'll never forget?

Listen to me, Lonely Radio, I sat behind you
in Spanish. Your hair kept changing colours—
black, purple, black, red, a beautiful lightshow.

Years later, an online boy you loved
was shot dead by his teenaged wife.
Another internet friend messaged you about it.

In the news article, you could see the wife's photo
but not his. Lonely Radio, you haven't written
in a while. I think of you every time I fly

from Terrace with Styrofoam coffee and the sun
closing red behind the mountains—please
write, please tell us that you're fine.

DRUNK RIVER

Instead of drunk driver, you wrote, *drunk
river*, and here you are back on the bank
of the Skeena, starring in some boy's sucky
idea of a first date: sitting silent in a truck
while a stranger weeps
through the radio, *Fuck Highway 16—
we want our girls back, our women.*
You know from every rest stop here
on south the girls and the women
want nothing more than to go back
to that staticky voice. And you know
they can't. They're somewhere
trapped. A hairy hand reaches over,
switches off the radio and the only weeping
now is your breathing in your teeth.
You think of the women and girls.
You think of the man and his pig farm.
On the news, you saw them, pink
snouts, squealing, eating up little bits,
the women, the girls. You think
of the women, the hairy hand, the pink
snouts, the girls, and you want to know
if you are pretty. Despite all the trouble
it causes, you want to know if you are pretty
here, tonight, in this truck beside this drunk river.
The hairy hand reaches over as if
to switch you off, too, but stops
on your knee trembling in knee sock.
After a second of windshield misting up
the hand slides up to the most pretty
girl bit of you. The hand pauses again a second.
And then lights a little match into you.

And you feel for a second second
like you won't wake up tomorrow
in your lilac bedroom, won't sit bored
in French class conjugating *Je voudrais
aller à l'université*. For a second maybe
there are no girls, no women wanting to go
home, they are home now, please, you
feel the skin of the moon on your face,
the river mist, which is the moon's finger
rubbing against you, wet and hot and
shivers, you feel holy hot and shivers,
you feel, slow down, slow down,
you feel holy and gorgeous, important,
maybe there is no boy here, no boy
who will drop you off after and make you
feel bad, no, no boy reeking in blue jeans
beside you, there is only you.
You know you will leave this place.
You have an itch, you breathe the mist
and wish you could rip it off like cotton
from the top of an Advil bottle: maybe
then there would be some relief.
And you would see the women and the girls
walking towards you, shrugging off
leather jackets, they'd say—they who are
so cool, beautiful and home now—
*I heard you on the radio at the mall. Pigs?
Don't be silly. You've been watching
too many horror movies. Help me unload
the car. Come see what I brought you.*

NARRATIVE THEORY

"A whole is that which has beginning, middle, and end."
　　—Aristotle

When did the hole in you begin?
Let's say you were fourteen
in the small silver room that was
your boyfriend's car, accelerating
towards the crest of the hill, his hand
riding the hem of your skirt.
Remember years earlier, when
your mom went to the hospital
for a week and you ate a brick
of cheese and watched your dad
stumble drunkenly between flowerbeds
that refused to flower. Kristie's voice
filtered in through your Minnie Mouse
fake rotary phone, telling you her sister
started cutting again. The two
of you—black eyeliner and vodka
Gatorade, panty drawers stocked
with Plan B and satanic CDs.
Your boyfriend, sucking
on your teeth in the Trigo's
parking lot, was bored of you.
Even you were bored of you.
Blistered with rain, his windshield
turned the streetlights into spider eyes.

At seventeen you fled with a suitcase,
thinking, *Thank you, Aristotle,*
this is the end of the hole. Now,
here's where I say, *Fuck Aristotle.*
The town still slouches into winter

every September, reemerging
the following June. Your memory
freezes and thaws again and again.
You return every year
on a twelve-passenger plane
that descends by spiralling around
an onion-shaped lake, woods
an Emily Carr retrospective,
a walloping green nausea.
Your ex says, *See you next
Christmas!* and you slam
his passenger door, plopping
snow from his wheel-well. You blow
smoke behind the North Star Bar,
while inside your dad retells
the same three stories—your life
less of the arc he expected and more
like a cedar growing in rings,
circling, circling.

BORN AGAIN

Sometimes a man will ask you to marry him
because he wants to keep your body
where he can see it. You were eighteen, newly
baptized and trying to wear your skin
so it looked brand new. Waving banners
in a church basement, you pretended
to be as pious as your new friends
who'd harmonized these hymns
since kindergarten. They gave you purity
journals, new translations,
whispered gibberish over you until you
grew holy with goosebumps.
Sometimes a man will ask you to marry him
because of the way you look
ladling chili for the congregation.
He'll sit intentionally in your pew, learn
your political views, claim you
hovered over him in a dream—a braid
of blue mist. He'll forgive you
your atheist father and ballroom dancing.

Sometimes a man asks you to marry him
and then rides away on a red motorcycle.
Last you heard, he'd knocked
up a receptionist in Prince Rupert,
was teaching orphans how to use power
tools. Sometimes it feels like a brick
sinking to the bottom of you remembering
the earnest way you waved him off
as he shrank to a dot on the highway.
You believed him when he said he felt
the call of the Lord, and would be back
in a year or two. Sometimes it feels

like you've shed your salvation—
watched it shrivel in the sun—new
skin fresh and itchy as a miracle.

ALUMINUM

A wet flag sliding up its pole
like a hunk of bread backwashed up a straw
is one way of saying everything
is disgusting if looked at a certain way.
Take the town you grew
up in, its three traffic lights
and skunk stench oozing up
from the gullies. Try to look at it
differently. Tell me the salmon sexing
to death in the Skeena are beautiful
in their pursuit of home, their black
spots just instinct's amorous fingerprints;
that the man three beers deep
running his dog alongside his pickup
on gravel roads is really
Walt Whitman and the salmon
are his silver beard dotted with pipe ash
and nostalgia. If you can tell me this
you're no longer looking
at Kitimat, but at a painting
hanging above your mother
in the German restaurant where you ate
schnitzel and buttered rolls, avoiding
her discussion of your future.
Try not to notice how grey she's gone
in this decade since you've lived with her,
her hair so many spawning salmon.
Look down at the parking lot; admire
Dairy Queen's most recent facelift,
a row of buildings for lease.
If the flag could dry enough to flap up
off its pole you'd see the snowflake logo
at its centre and a childhood feeling

of ok might spread like butter across you.
Look! There's Whitman strapping
his little boat to the roof of his truck,
his feet swimming in brown rain boots.
He is rearranging his fishing
tackle, readying to row off
onto the godawful water.

GIRL LIKE

A girl like you once sold her period panties
on the internet for eighty dollars plus shipping.

She quit the swim team to sleep more.

She thought she was the only girl to be softly
devastated on the back of a motorcycle, breathing in
his hair, highway-high in the hours between
curfew and the missing person's report.

A girl like you once knew how
to solve for *x* with calculator accuracy.

A girl like you once liked girls.
She sat on her bed lacing girl fingers together.
In the rose light from the glitter lamp,
her body looked factory-perfect.
She was like a Ouija board
hands ghosted over, spelling out
b-a-l-s-a-m, s-o-a-k, a-m-b-i-g-u-o-u-s.
A girl like you once haunted
that girl's skin for years.

Night settled its thick sediment inside
of a girl like you and no one whispered to her,
Darling, that feeling is just the gin
you had for dinner—you will survive
this night and many others.

If I had a nickel for every time a girl like you
couldn't buy a belt to hold up her end
of the story I could buy a belt with nickels.

A girl like you phoned TEEN HELPLINE
every afternoon for three months but never felt any better.

She couldn't say *algebra* without giggling.

Once she got an anonymous e-mail
calling her an arrogant cunt and got
arrogant cunt silk-screened onto a t-shirt.

Like so many girls, she watched her car
getting acne in the hailstorm of high-pressure feelings —
Quiet your heart, darling, it's only a car alarm.

A girl like you once took her rose quartz to the river
and threw it so hard into spring runoff she bruised a salmon.
Snails made the rocks wet with their bodies,
but when she returned home, her rose quartz was still
glowing on her windowsill and love still
pooled like pantyhose in her shoes.

It doesn't make any sense — lining your eyes
so deliberately before making strangers wet with your body.

She had her tit pics circulated by the hockey
team's boy god and tried to off herself,
stopped eating until she saw god
in the cliff face of Elizabeth Mountain.

I'm sorry I held your heart down
with the sole of my sneaker. Once a girl like you
did that to me when I thought she was just trying
to teach me how to hotwire a car.

She waited until university to google how
to masturbate because a body like hers
came sans instruction manual.

A girl like you once loved a boy but love
held her words hostage like a dog in a hot car
and no good Samaritan came along to crowbar her
windshield. *Darling, did your feelings suffocate?*

A girl like you blew all her money on a one-way
ticket to Ann Arbor to meet a twitter stranger
then refused to step onto the train.

Girls like you go around breaking in,
stealing strangers' jackets and wearing
them to bonfires. Darling, when a girl
like you busts you open, she will take
six dollars and twenty-three cents
and that mixtape you love more
than anything, but you will get over it.

A girl like you once drove her car
all the way down Elizabeth Mountain
silent except for her own dumb heart
and the catcall of wind in tall firs.
The cassette case sat on her dash,
useless as a corpse's shoe. She shoved it into
the glove box, that girl like you.
She got over it.

II

FUN AND GAMES

All I know about fun I learned pushing
playground pebbles down my ear canals
in preschool then shaking them
out at home alone in the bathroom.
Wonderful fun until one got stuck.
Another game I played
was how many panties could I get
away with wearing at one time
until my mother caught me
playing it in the Costco washroom.
Now the only game I play is losing
chess to Zaq. Every night
he assassinates my royal family.
Then we wash dishes. I don't think
I am getting any better at fun.
Our apartment sits atop
a nightclub and sometimes girls
mistakenly stumble up our stairs.
What fun their ankles seem to have,
rolling out from under them.

MICHELLE ON INSTAGRAM

I liked the photo of you eating.
I liked the photo of you stacking
your panties into a suitcase bound
for China. I did not like China.
Its unreliable wifi spaced out
your face until little of your face
remained in my life, but I liked
the photo of you and your turtle
in China. I tapped on its shell
twice with index finger, liked.
You with your students in China.
You at Chinese Disneyland with
your fiancé. You chewing god-
knows. The photo you took
of Paul Simon's cardstock cutout
wearing your army green parka. You
drunk-leaning on a balcony. I liked
Paul Simon. Vincent's ramen.
Your new apartment. That other
bitch you sometimes hang out with
who isn't Paul Simon. I liked
your wedding. Everyone crying
at your wedding. Double-tap.
I liked your wedding so much
along with hundreds of other
likers who liked your wedding.
Mimosas. Swans. Lasagna. It
happened so fast. Your mother,
your grandmother in coral, her hair
turned way up. Sorry for saying
I should've been a groomsman.
I liked the groomsmen. I tapped
on their faces. I like you in beer

league, swinging a bat through
Leo-season. Can you feel me tap
on your faces, liking your life?
Do you like your life? I like it
so much I make all the small
hearts underneath you light up.

SLEEPING IS THE ONLY LOVE

Lately I've seen your face fried
onto a whole lot of cheese sandwiches.
Spent several sad lunches traipsing
over your web presence. Links linked
me to your namesake, a patent
attorney living in Hillsboro, Ohio,
where a water tower looks lonelier
than you ever looked watching
an empty football field. Yesterday
a street band covered that Silver Jews
song, you know the one, and a boy's
back in the crowd looked like
your back, a life raft bobbing
in the ocean of a stranger. Above us
clouds cobbled together that look
you could never pull off and parted
to a cool nothingness like the concave
theatre inside my skull where you
are projected—an image my brain
flips upside down to flip right side up—
where I rebroadcast that morning
your room reeked of multivitamins
and I ran weeping down Cook Street,
seagulls heaped like Kleenex on the curb.
Today my Kleenex are inedible popcorn
pieces, yet even in their crumpled
nothing shapes I see your face.

SALMON AND POTATO SALAD

Matthew, I am stretching the Os
in your poems into lifesavers
so grey daily moments don't drown me.
Now I am running my fingers
cautiously along the underside
of my studio chair to assess the grossness
of its previous owner until I realize *teas*
sounds like *tease* and feel a ping.
In Toronto you are steaming
milk in metal pitchers while your mind
grows a book of potato poems.
I listen to printmakers argue
over whether or not to buy
chocolate bars or continue printing books
so trendy you don't even read them.
I move three words up a line
then back down. Matthew, the bathroom
in this place is like the setting
of a Chuck Palahniuk short story
in which bad things happen
to your body so that the reader
passes out. Megan says there's a
second bathroom if I don't want
to encounter art on the toilet.
I don't want to encounter much of anything
on the toilet, especially nothing
sculpted by snacky voices past
yon partition. Every afternoon I watch
several of them in too-short
sweatpants pour the communal
kettle onto mugs of noodles.
How much like fishing poetry
is, casting lines until something

larger bites—I hardly have time
to zip my jeans, exit the art
and scribble that down before
my brain flushes the bowl.
Once I reeled in a salmon to shore
but was too afraid of its teeth
to stick my hand into its gill and lift it.
In the photo, I stand grinning
beside my father, who dangles
its rainbow belly beside my head.
I really miss him. Things happen
and I don't know how they go together
but neither do you, sculpting swans
out of hot foam and poems out of the rocky
soil of your youth. I've never lifted a fish.
The voices shrink on their way to chocolate
like a memory growing too old
to remember what it ate for breakfast.
Someone says, *Where did Matthew go?*
Who does that guy think he is?
I'm not totally sure I know
who I think you are anymore or what
I'm doing in this city I can't afford
and that you've left. You text me
a photo of beautiful iridescent pigeons
and I'm dragged back to shore.

MONEY

Last night at a book launch
in Toronto Aisha Sasha John
read, *I need a lot of money.*
I like that because I need money
too but it's like an aunt
once told everyone it was tacky
to admit it. Why is not dying
so embarrassing? Imagine
getting all the money required
to live through the calendar
as one wad of twenties.
I like twenties because
they're wearing the Queen.
How many twenties would
you need and what else? I'd need
a lot of tampons to avoid
just bleeding onto the streets.
Also I need a lot of people
around who call me
the correct name. I need
Angela and a bucket of coffee.
Most of what we do isn't living—
it's laundry, it's operating
a can opener, it's passing
beautiful people on the street
then never seeing them again.
Or meeting them and discovering
they're awful on the inside.
Some mornings I read really
interesting articles about shit
in Bangladesh, Wisconsin,
or deep in the tissue papers
of the gorilla heart, and some

afternoons I don't remember
any of it. This can't be living.
Last night between hellos
with literary near-strangers
I stood beside Michelle
and the feeling of really
living crushed through me
like a ghost elephant lowering
its ghost feet and impeccable
ghost memory onto my skeleton,
and I wondered if everyone
or even just Michelle
could tell I was crying.

VORTEX FLUID DEVICE

In California, chemists are "unboiling" eggs
to cure children and vaccinate cancer.
I am unwriting poems, letter by letter,
to cure sentimentality because Benjamin
quit writing and what is any of us
doing if he's not out there ghosting
the language? What an awful way to talk
to someone you don't talk to anymore—
write a poem and maybe he'll get it.
Of course I'm too selfish to unwrite
my poems. Everything I say in poems is
a lie—even that—and what are you gonna do
about it? The English language has
between 0.6 and 1.3 bits of entropy
per character of message, meaning
I'm predictable, meaning here's where
I tell you my father taught me long
division with a mechanical pencil on
the cardboard core of a toilet paper roll.
The Californian chemists have clean names
like Gregory and Stephen. They have
made expensive hamster ovary options
obsolete by doing something I don't
understand involving a vortex fluid device
that unfolds proteins. You might think
this means we can go back to before
the egg was cracked, the two of us
famished in your kitchen with sleep-grit
in our tear ducts and maybe—instead
of what happened—a *Jumanji* stampede
of wildebeest will mash our proteins
into your linoleum. Or maybe we go
to Wannawafel for waffles and never

have that fight. You might think this, but the entropy of the universe still increases, said one of the scientists in an interview.

NAANWICH WAS THE LAST THING

Do you remember the baseball diamond
beside which we ate naanwich, Liz?
It tasted nothing like butter chicken.
We'd wandered all morning without eating,
our hunger revealing to us the aggression
of nearby seagulls. I loved your light
lisp, your dangling St. Christopher,
how you softly smelled of vegetable broth.
I loved your amateur and terrifying
taxidermy, your slack rabbit.
Naanwich was the last thing we ate
before you said we couldn't stay friends.
Today I watched it rain and rain
never turning any less grey.
I thought of ways I'd kiss the girl
I like in a taxi or an alley. I dreamed
of train trips with married poets
to romantic American cities. I thought
of you. Of your perfect Lord kissing
you on the forehead with a tenderness
absent from my sordid ordinary life.
You drew a church in His glory, painted it
a holy purple people misinterpreted
as burning. But I think it *was* burning.
I think you were, too. The last poem
I wrote about you came to me also
during Lent, this grey space that blows
wind and guilt straight through me.
A hymn sticking in my throat like dry wafer.
I still feel the warm thumbs of priests
on my head reminding me I am nothing.
Wait, you said, *that's not all of it.*
You are nothing "if you are

not loved." On shitty white bleachers
beside a baseball diamond you said
you could no longer love me.
Teenagers passed us kicking wet stones.
You couldn't love me. Then you turned
up your hood and walked away,
away into safe and tender burning.

SELFIE

I asked Zaq to show me where we are
in the milky swirl. *Here,* he said, pointing to something

nebulous on his screen, and it felt
like searching a first-trimester ultrasound photo

for its heart, pretending I see it too, the tiny life inside
chaotic dark. We are simultaneously moving

towards and away from a black hole at the centre
of our galaxy. We are a bug

on the windshield of a tank gunning along
the Autobahn. *Even smaller,* Zaq says.

The bug that bug had for lunch, if that.
It's sad being the bug other bugs nom on.

Even sadder is the fact there aren't any
other bugs—no one

complicit in our spinning. It's just us.
I lied when I said Zaq and I live

above a nightclub. It's a thrift store and anyway
we don't even live there anymore.

When I ran out of clean clothes
I'd grab a shirt off the discount rack and smell

like a stranger all day. It shrunk
my loneliness, I like to think, living like that.

We got lost by the salmon-shaped lantern school
watching lantern roe hatch into tadpole candles
and arrive transfixed in a field of lantern wheat.
A lantern thought bubble above your head says maybe
we could hold hands inside your jacket pocket.

We follow the crowd looking up directions
on their lantern phones. Great horned owl lantern.
Lantern Hamlet lecturing his unlit skull. A bouquet
of carnations in lantern colours. A lantern your niece
made out of a soup can, three nails, and her feelings.

A lantern I just wrote. A woman plucks a harp
behind an illuminated nativity scene—which half
is the lantern? Two tweenage lanterns kissing.

An electric lantern shaped like nothing in itself
emits silhouettes of geese and sighs of mothers upon
seeing your recent piercings. Their lantern book
club has just uncorked another Malbec.

A man drizzling food colouring on a projector
is a sort of lonely man-lantern growing cold
in a field of impatient children. Impatient
children in neon windbreakers are excellent
lanterns and continue burning past bedtime.

Lantern shaped like that ugly thing I said
at breakfast—quit looking at it. Lantern lime
as a hangover, crying into the garburator.
A lantern says, *It's your turn to do the dishes.*
Another says, *Let's leave them 'til tomorrow.*

Historical lantern figures we've looked up at
since childhood. You photograph me between
Gertrude and a flying pig. Little boat who brought
my dad to Canada—float on that ocean of light
a while longer, ferrying souls to safer shores.

Click-bait lantern and us crowded around waiting
for kittens and life-hacks to load. It's too shiny
and aimed at us. I just want to carve a face
onto an orange vegetable with you, a big
crooked grin with three teeth, but I know
we'll leave it to rot on the stoop until February.

There's nothing like a lantern to make us guilty
about our many moods. There's nothing like a lantern.
Even in the hail it sits in its same face, even
when I say, *You're a real asshole,* it glows.

It's ok, you say. *We're just lanterns waiting*
for a volunteer's hands to place candles inside us—
then the crowd might huddle in our light.
Though we're half-collapsed by the rain we'll look
more human for it, our faces clumsily papered.
Even though you're a real asshole, you'll glow.

III

BUOYANT CRAFT

You told me the epistolary form broke
your silence, Kyla, so here I go writing
to you. Last night at the restaurant
where I work lifting so many beer glasses
off tables—each of them filled
with filmy hay-bale light—I realized
I am seventeen percent in love
with you and only Shaun knows.
He thinks it's "cute" because you don't
have a dick. By cute I of course mean
nonthreatening. At the beginning
of *I Love Dick* by Chris Kraus
Dick has slept or is sleeping or has failed
to sleep with some bimbo named Kyla.
At his ranch in Antelope Valley
we hear Kyla fumble through an apology
inside a shroud of static while Dick hangs
impotently out. What if, instead of Dick,
Chris'd written letters to Kyla, the way
I am writing to you, Kyla, through
the text memo setting on my iPhone 4,
hundreds of pages to a female stranger
whose voice Chris only overheard via
an accident of the answering machine age.
In Gaelic, Kyla means *strait*.
Sometimes I think I need a kind
of buoyant craft to navigate you
but it's only my not-so-straight self
I can't handle. Once a boy drove
sixteen hours across Canadian January
to visit me, then decided not to date me.
In his own *I Love* story I was
the Dick he'd met at a party,

years earlier, a disappointing figment
he'd shone his twenty-one-year-old
narcissism onto. Of course Dick means
king and *strong*. In this way, Kyla,
you are all the dick I'll ever need.

MY TEETH ARE TOMBSTONES WITH YOUR NAME
ENGRAVED ON THEM

I am standing in a cemetery
eating a breakfast burrito, Kyla.
In its aesthetic wisdom the city
irrigates this cemetery by pumping
water through black tubes
so that our dead, however
problematically they lived
(god rest them), will reincarnate
as big dead trees with burgundy
rotting blossoms. Don't worry, Kyla—
I know how death works. I know
as much as any living human
eating her breakfast burrito
in a cemetery does, which is zilch,
not even if these eggs have loitered
too long in what's known
as "danger zone" and grown toxic.
I'm trying to say I worry about
dying. I worry about my fertility,
about hurting Shaun and not doing enough
about microaggressions I notice on buses.
Beautiful women keep running
past me with beautiful sad faces
and sometimes panting well-bred
beautiful sad dogs. I know they will
outlive me by five minutes
for each kilometre they can manage
to lap our problematic dead.
It might even be worth it
to be beautiful and sad
if it means I get to live a few
minutes, maybe hours, longer

writing poems to you in this
erotically blossoming city
with good coffee shops.

VENTI THREE-PUMP-CLASSIC NONFAT EASY-WATER EXTRA-HOT AMERICANO MISTO*

And isn't gender sad, to not fit into the Christmas dress? To bunch at constructs. Because my father told me I was brilliant over 7-11 Slurpees on a not infrequent basis I like to believe I'm exempt but I, too, chafe at the edges. I am enormous in my flopping female want. I still cry into the *Joy of Cooking* and flashbacks of my tiny grandmother folding towels in the late southern Albertan mornings. I wanted to say "mournings," to say the light those mournings was a mixture of dryer lint and wildflower honey. My coffee is bitter with the cinnamon and gendergrief I've mixed into it. Still I keep sipping. And I know you understand, Kyla, and are somewhere sipping this with me, before zipping into the girl uniform and wandering the world as if *she* fits.

*drink ordered by a different Kyla at the Starbucks I once worked at

THIS IS GARBAGE!

People say you can't play
on both teams, so go home.
They say, *Smile.* They say
you're lying to impress men.
They whistle from windows.
People say (is there no end
to what they say?), *Tell us
more about this Kyla person.*
I met you in journalism class
and once tried to feed you
Chinese takeout in bed
with this guy I was dating.
You modelled as a teenager.
Your hair was blonde when
we met and now it's not.
And now I'm using you
to talk about my baggage
because you always open
bags of people's garbage
and say, *This is garbage!*
while I hang air freshener
and say, *Maybe this is ok,*
when it is truly garbage.
People always call me *Kyla,*
so it's like I'm talking
to myself when I say people
say you're so straight.
The last time I saw you
we held hands before you read
your beautiful micro-poems.
They blossomed like daisies
before fly-trapping the face
of every bro in the room.

I hope people like them,
but people think bags upon
bags of garbage, so maybe
the meaning of this poem is
fuck what people think,
Kyla—you're killing it.

EEL

In LA a Canadian poet told me
I had too many panties on. *All of your idols
will topple like Jenga towers,*

our friend Chris said while holding my hand
in one of the badly carpeted nowhere
corridors of the JW Marriott.

Then I sauntered off wearing excessive
panties to kiss the poet
in a glass elevator. Now I am

eating zesty ranch in-flight
snacks on my way back to Canada
and they dissolve in me

like the few shits I still give
about my reputation. I slip the empty
metallic package into the mesh seatback.

The in-seat screen winces
onto the Discovery Channel, where men
toss king crabs into unknowable

starboard and port holes. The crabs
vanish like a colleague's love
interest from the peripheries

of a social circle. We never get to ask
what happened or hear her
version. When I kissed the poet

I didn't know about his girlfriend
or how to find my Hollywood hotel.
When the poet's hands dipped

below denim, I didn't notice
it was ego, not romance, that slithered
around in me like an eel. When I went

to LA, I knew only how to drop traps
and watch my own face waver
in the wake of the cage.

I think the only important work
is finding a way to be ok crying
in cafés. In Our Town, "Fernando"
by ABBA is playing and it's shitty
how fleeting being in LA at AWP
with you was. Every minute at least
eight new ideas blew my thinking.
From an internet distance, I watched
Adèle (our friend not the singer)
froth in a yellow muumuu and crash.
For me LA was reenacting *Labyrinth*
with a Canadian poet I admired
and knowing I am only beginning
to find something I can move around
in and call *my voice*. It's hairy
and complicated and I want it
to be uppercase all the time even
though that's audacious. So I can't stop
ugly-crying alone at a table for four
and no I won't go to the BC Book
Prize soiree tonight — that sounds awful.
I might go glow bowling
with coworkers from the nerd bar.
Part of my current important crying
work borrows a stranger's pencil
and underlines lines in Ariana Reines'
Coeur de Lion. The first: *It is difficult
to know anything.* You were right
in your poem, Kyla: Canada is cold,
so careerist it often says nothing,
but *there was something in the air
that night* when the LA light turned
the palm leaves into ribbons ripped

from our childhood cassettes. Music
floated down and for a moment it felt
like we could say and finally mean
something. It's embarrassing what
disco does to me and I don't even really
like music or know if you do either.

AND DON'T EVER FUCKING STOP

I wanted to put so many more things
in those LA poems. Like how you felt
unbeautiful and up for summer fucking
and how I can't stop fucking
this bartender I work with. I mean
we were trying to put clothes on
earlier and I bent over a little
and we just started up again.
It's getting absurd. About that dress
you hated, Jane said, *Kyla looks better
in that potato sack than I ever will.*
Later you had changed into black
denim and asked me if I was going
to the dance, but I was hungover
from Claudia Rankine's keynote
urging me to revise my entire life.
I slept for eleven hours and woke
up copacetic in Hollywood.
Of course I think you're beautiful
but not in the way people used
to pay you to be. I want to explain
in some way that won't make either of us
angry or uncomfortable, but that
would mean having to define
beauty and who has the time?
I can only say thinking about you
made me purchase a coffee mug
in Portland with Cheryl Strayed's
WRITE LIKE A MOTHERFUCKER
quote emblazoned on it.
It's on my bookshelf and I keep
forgetting to give it to you.

FINNISH SCHOOLING

I texted you, "Finnish
Schooling," and I'm sorry
if you took it as a command.
You've been out
of school for years
and are quite finished.
I meant the educational
system in Finland.
I saw a thing
on it once—no, not
a documentary, just one
of those things that pops
up when you are passing
statuses and photos
and all the other cut-up bits
of their lives people
put on the internet.
In Finland kids are
so happy. They don't
have homework. They
read Ishiguro novels
while whittling cedar
computers, oblivious
to the gold medals
they're getting in every
international category.
Today I thought of them
again while having
a fast food taco
in my girlfriend's Hyundai.
We were driving back
to Canada from Portland
and didn't want to

stop for lunch. I bet
Finnish children stop
for lunch even if
it means longer wait
times at the border.
You had an idea
that we could get tech
bros to pay us to give
motivational talks
about poetry and
creativity. Then they
would feel creative
and poetic like they just
bought a sexy coffee
table book, a big one
with glacier photos.
And we would have
money, which is just
what we need. I used to hate
money but have come
to terms with needing it.
You see I need to insert it
into my life in order
for the poems
to come out. If I don't,
only death dispenses.
You were so excited,
drinking red wine
on the patio, vibrating
with all the ways
we might not die
like a brilliant giant
Finnish child. I was thinking
we could tell
the tech bros about
the Finnish system.

That's what I meant
to text you. We could
tell them there is
a place where
kids don't choose
between being poets
and being tech bros.
We could ask them
to design a system
that lets us feel
like that, free and lathered
in many green
breezes from the north.

GOOD WITHOUT THE GUACAMOLE

Last night I went to the restaurant
where your boyfriend briefly worked
and ordered the nachos—does anyone order

anything else there? I asked for a side
thing of guacamole, but they'd run out.
They have a full menu but they're known

for nachos. In restaurant lingo, a side thing
of guacamole is known as a ramekin
of guacamole. Is it just me or does

ramekin sound like what we do to our dead
in cemeteries after we tenderly enclose them
in their coffins? Your boyfriend was so beautiful

you might not think he'll get ramekinned into
some cemetery, but sure as your already
half-ramekinned great aunt Gladys, he will.

The nachos were even good without the guacamole,
like how salad tastes like salad without dressing
but you might miss the vinegar a little.

*

Your briefly beautiful boyfriend wore
the following tattoos: a kind of honey
donut on his ribs, a palm tree,

the words TOO SOBER, and a teepee
he regrets, which he could probably turn into
a bat. (Sorry, I just invented those tattoos

because you stopped responding
to my increasingly creepy texts
about your boyfriend, but I do remember you

saying his tattoos were bizarre. It's amazing
what briefly beautiful humans can get
away with.) I'm sorry, as well, that we haven't

talked in months and that I texted you
out of nowhere about your boyfriend.
I know you really hate that shit. I tried

texting you "me'n'u" but my phone
corrected it to "menu." Back at the restaurant
my own briefly boyfriend and I were getting

so slowly smashed off grapefruit shandy
that the staff's fashion changed
several times while we camped in our corner

table bordered by giant windows.
That place only employs the most
beautiful and stylish young people or else

they get 86 real fast. (86 in restaurants is when
you're out of something, like guacamole.)
You might say, *I'm all 86 love;*

I'm so 86 you. When humans are 86,
we ramekin them into the dirt
all pretty burrito-wrapped in their coffins.

*

I don't know what to do in the interlude

between now and the 86-to-ramekin
portion of my existence. I used to

set schedules. I planted some beans
last week—got two degrees—and hope
they poke up. For some, it's about getting

as much side-guacamole as possible,
by which I mean cars and a house, maybe
some kids. Nadine's friend's sister got a ton

of cavities when she was pregnant
which kind of put me off having kids.
Plus months of barfing and overpopulation

and the fear they will pre-86 you.
Other people go around like chicken
burritos pretending pork burritos

aren't burritos and write books about it
and go on TV turning real "hot salsa," spitting
everywhere. Some other other people

say can't we get along—we're all just
burritos, after all. I just want to sit with friends
in restaurants or wherever for as long

as possible laughing about our bad tattoos
and brief boyfriends, ignoring the service
and the food—cooling and congealing

long into the evening—until
they turn on "Closing Time,"
until they show us to the dirt.

Kyla, Stats Canada keeps calling me.
They leave messages
saying I should call them back.
Like some boy I met at a club once
Stats Canada just can't comprehend
rejection, but if there's one thing
I've learned from living on this earth
for nearly thirty years it's how
to ghost. My father taught me.
And his father taught him.
Am I single, married, widowed,
divorced? Do I make over
twenty-five grand annually?
It's how they sort people.
It's boring, so I won't answer.
Stats Canada are the worst
ice breakers. A better line
of inquiry would be to ask
how many people I've ghosted.
0–5, 5–10, 10+. And how often
do I think about them? Always,
sometimes, rarely, never.
I'm slumped on my bed
at my mom's house sometimes
thinking of my ghostees
going about regular living.
One in particular I like to imagine
sitting on a bench scrolling
through Instagram with her hair
flapping like a crow. I didn't ghost
you, Kyla. We just drifted apart
like lily pads. Most of the time
when my father called me

I didn't answer and when I called
him back he answered in an *uh-huh*
ghosting way. And now he is dead.
Will Stats Canada die too
if I ghost them long enough?
Then will they ghost me
like a real ghost? I mean haunt.
Like my father is haunting me.
I mean metaphorically
but also I can't sleep
because this house keeps
coughing the way my father did
when he lived and still smoked—
the phlegm sounded
like a root with no end
that grew all the way through
the very bottom of him.

GOODBYE KYLA

Kyla, it was kind
of you to get me
that necklace that resembles
a moustache. Whenever
I wear it people say,
Nice moustache. To me
it looks more like
a child's drawing
of a seagull—a black wax
squiggle on indigo
construction paper.
This afternoon I emailed
myself an article
about how to reduce
stress in the body.
You know I will
never read it—
stress will continue
to accumulate
inside my body
like gunk in a vent.
Because my family and I
burned my dad's body
stress no longer
accumulates inside him.
My body has inherited it.
It's not true I'll never
read that article.
I read it immediately
and have decided
to move to an island
where I will wear
that necklace

you gave me and sit
in damp sand.
Remember when dads
shaved and we cried
at stranger dads?
It was like that, but we
also shaved off his body
and bones, his voice
and bear hugs.
His body stopped
being a place.
But the sea is still a place.
The island is a place
where moustaches hover
on the sky above the sea.
They are so free
of stress they are
floating. Just hanging
out on the sky.
The sky must have
so many friends, it has
such an excellent
collection of necklaces.

IV

BEER INTERVIEW

My flight of beers looks like six bulbs
plugged into a wooden fixture. The first,
a lager, is late August at dusk, smog-orange.

Next, the nut-brown barley light
of lake bottom. I sip sunrise, hiding
from cousin David in grandma's hayloft.

I lift each feeling like a giant and dim
it with my lips. You tap your recorder,
wake it to collect what I say. I take winter

ale from its socket, sip the snow's blue
lining, tell you how where I grew up
the snow piled thick enough

to die in. I lift running illuminated
by stadium lights after sundown, the brief
dandelion summer I ran every second

day, thinking I'd one day sprint
into a different city. That amber week
I spent my evenings retrieving

my father from the casino—my voice
leaks into your device—I will not
drink that light, so thick with sediment.

Nor will I drink the black-lit backhand
of God that crashed through me
on the aluminum bridge where I stood

trying to throw my life down the throat
of the Kitimat River. It had rained
sideways for so many days I'd forgotten

what was up. When I saw a porcupine dragging
her poncho of quills along the highway
of tears I began my stumbling home.

I was sick for six weeks, so sick
I hallucinated northern lights. I'm sorry,
what did you ask? Yes, I'm finished.

PLACEBO, NUNAVUT

Every morning my morning
hope fades failing the crossword.
What's a seven-letter word
for sugarpill that begins
with this low-belly dread?
Perilous wind bisects QC abbr
for corner store and I know
neither. What percentage
of thrift store treasures belong
to someone's dead relative?
Daylight sifts through my desk,
dribbles between fern curls.
Province of Chesterfield Inlet.
Antonym of airborne. Third
cup of coffee from the BEST
GRANDPA mug, wondering when
he last used it or anything.
Five-letter layabout. Trout basket.
A crow crash-lands in the eaves.
Soon a panic at near-lateness
that to others resembles purpose
will lift me from this red
wheelie chair and fling me
ignorant into the streets.
Ends with an A. Steady tap
of pen cap on newsprint,
sipping from this cup I gave
my grandfather and that his death
gave back to me. That itch
where the limb fit. Never again
will he mention its chipped
rim before upturning it
to drip-dry beside the sink.

THE NEWSPAPERS

Before unlocking the café, I lift
the newspapers off the curb and hug them
to my chest like they were the first children
born today. They smell like the final
lumps of grey snow in April, the undersides
of semi-trailers—they smell like 5AM.
5AM smells like hugging them
while locking myself inside a café
that doesn't open for another half hour.
I roll their rubber bands off, stack them
on wire racks, brew coffee, unwrap
and arrange banana bread, lemon loaf,
shift from foot to foot testing balance
and consciousness. I love these
brief moments with the blueberry muffins,
the coffee grinder clearing its throat
before anyone enters demanding coffee.
On my break, I'll twist the rubber bands
onto my rubber band ball, working
its diameter above an inch and wonder
how early the carrier wakes to hurl
the day's news at our door, what
she does on her break from the grey
bundles of papers arcing through pre-dawn
dark, their cold thump onto the curb.

TESTICULONIMBUS

I hate clouds they're always
spitting in my americanos
looking somewhat but not
exactly like childhood pets
whose afterlives my parents
lied about. The better place
Bronco went was the dirt
under our butter lettuce, better
indeed than with our sorry lot
who robbed him of his beloved
testicles. Little white liars
who promise rain but don't
deliver until you're wrecked
on margaritas in a flimsy dress
trying to send a text message.
Testicles from the Latin
testiculus meaning witnesses.
Testiculonimbus hang low
on the horizon, presiding over
sex shops where dildos bear
no witness. They look about
to cry then like candy floss
they blow apart to form
an elsewhere dragon. Could
it be ok to be something else
clouds make me wonder,
to float a little calmly eastward?
But when I fall I don't tickle
foreheads of kissing couples.
I don't feed fields of canola.
I rip my knees and the sky
won't lift me back up again.

DEATH STARRING WINONA RYDER

Her eyes are the three faces of Cerberus.
The third hides behind her shocked bangs.
No, the third is her pursed mouth. If you zoom
in on Winona you will see her skin
is filled with third eyes—we call them pores.
Each one of them is rolling. Each one
of them a head to the dog guarding Death.
Of course an actor covered in third eyes
that also guard Death would be difficult
to work with. What did you expect?
She has the most magical acne. You may feel
her whole body making eye contact with you
because it is, but mostly her whole body
has better things to look at like very
long trains and sexy rivers. If the dogs
guard Death then inside of her is where
all the dead people live. All the living people
live outside of her eating pretzels etc. like
you and me. Wow, she is extremely
haunted. Ever thought *Beetlejuice* felt
a bit too same-same to your home movies?
Me too. All our Ouija boards call
out Winona during sex over and over.
It would be boring if it wasn't Winona.
Don't call her a bitch though she is covered
in bitches and sometimes they are in heat.
Sometimes you can smell her skin—it smells
like it just ran into the yard and murdered
something so quickly you didn't even hear it
die, but when Winona dies what happens?
What will happen to us when Winona dies?

BIBLIOPHILIA

I am very avant-garde in what
I use for bookmarks. That
look on your face would do.
A clump of my hair in a pinch.
At sixteen I dumped
coffee into Jane Austen
and still she crackles open
on a botched proposal.
I am a monster dogearer.
I use Joan Didion as a napkin.
Before I became a person
my dad lived on a farm
with no electricity, only
Louis L'Amour for toilet paper.
So it is my birthright to defile
the printed word. Instead
of depositing my book
into my bag when my hands
are doing other things
like masturbating or thumbing
avocados I dangle it
from my teeth like a retriever
presenting her retrieved.
If you love something so much
why do you keep it
up on that shelf and never
touch it? It's like you want
a virgin wife while all
I want is a girl I can bend
backwards over tombstones,
lick Pringles from her cracks

and cackle with. We stay
up all night with séances
and french-braiding and neither
of us ever wears white.

UNDER CONSTRUCTION

You'd think that empty lot
had slaughtered their mothers
the way those men torture it
with yellow machines. With how
little sleep you've been
getting, you think a lot
of sinister things, especially
these mornings when light
is the translucent grey
of fake teeth. Your dad
used to bring you home
dinosaur bones from the foothills
he razed to lay highways.
You can't remember when
you realized trucks run
on a broth of ancient lizards
but now they'll never not
feel haunted. It's important
to get places but you doubt
another condo tower
beside the train line
will do more than rattle
like a Yahtzee cup tossing
professional couples.
You keep the fossils
like jewelry on your dresser,
stroke their tar settings
until they look wet. A view,
more sleep, a new life
with fewer machines —
you've wanted so
much for so long you
don't remember living

without the fuel light on.
An invisible raptor stands
behind you in a business
suit, factoring in inflation
with his talon on your hand.

TECH SUPPORT

I have turned the thingy off and on, off
and on. I have bonked the thingy
with my hand and other doodads. So as
to dislodge dust, I have blown into
the thingy, while lifting it above my head
to gawk its problem from below.
I have imitated the various whirring
and beeping noises articulated prior
to the malfunction. To no fewer than six
male voices on EXT. 422 have I loudly
complained about these failings, receiving
intricate coughs in response. I have (over
wine) confided intimate information
to appeal to its emotions and then abused
it with numerous expletives including,
but not limited to, variations of "to shit,"
"to fellate," and "to fornicate mother."
I have phoned the 1-800 number and held on.
I have purchased the extended warranty.
I have pushed and slid the components,
as if performing a massage, plunged
a toothpick into "reset," waited thirty seconds,
and withdrawn said toothpick. I have
performed a séance over the thingy,
contacting its grandfather, the telegraph,
who responded in rhythmic clicks,
Have you tried turning it off and then on?

TENDER LIKE BEVERLY TENDER

All anyone ever wants to hear about
is the dinosaur erotica I wrote for the nerd bar
I work at. I can't remember how I was asked

to write *Wet Hot Allosaurus Summer* to be sold
in vending machines under the Millennium
Falcon. Many events seem arbitrarily arrived at

and when one begins to doubt the whole concept
of narrative, it can be hard to imagine
a convincing rising action between Tanis,

a lonely farm girl, and a ripped, impossibly
resurrected Allosaurus named Big Al,
who works on oil rigs. It can suck

your tank empty, not knowing how
moments connect, as they seem randomly
suspended in amber. Tanis sits in anticipation

on her tin roof and Big Al stares
at his footprints in the mud, wondering
when they will fossilize like this plot.

The first part of my life was a prehistoric
bug. The second part was a second
prehistoric bug. More life, more bugs

crushed on the windshield. Bug marmalade
under the wipers. The part of my life
I spent writing dinosaur erotica is encased

in honey resin. It was senseless and lovely

like buying textbooks online while
someone you love eats you out.

Possible it seemed to layer an Escape
from New York Sour by night and, rolling up
one's hair into the solemn knot of the erotic

novelist, then wake and type the word *throbbing*—
to feel one's typing fingerprints
throbbing, to call one's self something

tender like Beverly Tender, and research
what Big Al's throbbing member may
have looked like, if it arced and how.

COPPER KOI

My heart can barely spell
arrhythmia but still inflates
my fingers. A day like any other—
my hair worries my scalp
and I want to know what
skin is made of. What wets
my mouth? Since learning
I harbour a uterus
I've been afraid of it
popping. Maybe while walking
or downward dog. Or when
our bodies play towards
one body. Maybe it's more
like a fish bobbing
in a small pond—copper
koi in the moon basin. Let me
cross this avenue lit with cherry
blossoms. Let me forget
pints of blood circling
my bones like nervous dogs.
On grandma's farm, I spent
entire afternoons lifting
cats, blissfully unaware of
the uterus flickering in me.
I believed if you cracked
me open, I'd be filled
with caramel or else
soft and hollow as a doll.

INVENTORY

Sometimes the bartenders fill shot glasses
until the liquid bubbles above the rim
and it's impossible to lift them without dripping.

I deliver these shots without telling my tables
what's been lost, for surely it's understood
something always spills in the distance

between people. In relationships, I've lost
so many books my shelves are starting
to look toothless. I lost my mood en route to

lunch and don't know if it was you or me
or my hunger who misplaced it. We fill
spillage sheets, tracking the constant small

losses, and adjust our inventory. My first entry
records the morning my parents drove
my beloved objects and me permanently

to a new province. I craved a yellow endless
horizon and woke daily to soggy mountains.
I requested mayo and got spread

relish instead. I'm still waiting,
Kyra Demski, for my clip-on earrings
and afternoons by Lakelse holding hands.

Permanently out of stock are my brave
face and phony orgasm. It's been ages
since I've considered reordering them.

MOSQUITOES

My grandmother, who sat
half her life on a porch
in northern Alberta
far from the Budapest
of her youth, collected
Styrofoam from under
supermarket meat
because it felt so
soft and precious,
scrubbed and stacked
it in the shed—shelves
and shelves of it. No one
knew what to do with it
after she died. My father
says she unwrapped
garlic and popped it
like hard candy, says
she smelled so bad
even the mosquitoes
wouldn't go near her—
and did I remember
those mosquitoes
big as nickels?

My father says I'm lucky
I'm not Hungarian
because I'd only be four
feet tall and no teeth.
He's converted
to Canadian and I'm his
so I'm Canadian. He laughs
when I say Canada
is stolen, that we should

return it to the lost
and found. He says
he found it, so it's his.

I don't know what
it is to wake up
one morning and run
for months, sleep in
ditches, eat bread
with worms in it, board
a ship captained
by strangers whose words
you can't understand
and then to sit on a train
for days waiting
until someone calls
your name. Wherever
they called your name
that's where you lived.
Even if mosquitoes
eclipsed the sun, winter
bit, and blackberries
grew tart as rhubarb,
that's where you lived.
My father was five
when they called
his name in Edmonton.
My grandmother,
twenty-three.

I don't know what it's like
for your father never
to visit or send Christmas
cards. I never moved out
at fifteen or lived broke
and naked on beaches.

I never hitchhiked without
teeth through my twenties
wondering where I'd eat,
stacking peanut butter
and blackberry jam on toast
until the diner closed down.
My father taught me
math and racism and he
loved me very much.
He taught me money
and aliens inventing
the pyramids. He
showed me how to act
like my grandmother
who acted like a man
so men wouldn't fuck her
over so often. He taught
me to be (sic) Canadian.
I left home at seventeen
with scholarships and his
chequing account. I left
Kitimat at seventeen fat
and healthy and loved.

I had to move to Victoria
to read *Monkey Beach*
and write an essay on Eden
Robinson's landscape
to understand what Kitimat
meant. Now when people
shrug when I say where
I'm from I ask if they've read
her or folded old pizza
slices in Alcan foil.
I am still waiting
for the master's degree

to sink in and make me
feel less like an Alcan
girl. Derrida Derrida
Derrida Heidegger
Sara Ahmed—I still love
city malls and escalators
and not running into
a friend's mom
every three blocks.
I love Superstore. I got
so happy I nearly died
at a food court in Honolulu.
Is that enough affect
theory for you? Halfway
through a book gala
I realized my dress
was on backwards.

I am still writing this cliché
Canadian shit. I am writing
dogwood and diaspora
along the lonely shoulders
of Coastal mountains.
Sorry I'm so boring.
Does what sustains me
have to be invasive
as blackberries choking
out native species?
Does it have to come
wrapped in so much
packaging? If I belong
anywhere, if I could
claim any space,
if I call my own
name here in this poem
could I live here?

What's the rent like
in my own poem?
Do I get a discount
for it being so
goddamn haunted?

I am trying to teach
a man who believes
he came here with
nothing and earned his
house and car and hates
thinking people don't
work as hard as he does
but get more, whose mother
worked as a teenager
in coalmines and died
of it at seventy. She grew
cancers the way a bush
bursts with blackberries.
I'm trying to tell a man
who worked for sixty
of his sixty-six years
and who financed my youth
and early adulthood
that I don't believe
work measures
a person. When people
ask me how to say
my surname I say it
the Canadian way.

Grandmother—I have eaten
such blackberries
balanced on the lips
of beautiful people.
Dead into a second

decade, you are peonies
and windowsill
dust, a wrinkle
in the milk, a late
morning ache. *There*
are moments when
the body is as
numinous as words,
says Robert Hass
in that blackberry poem
everybody loves.
Grandmother, your flat
feet, your temper and red
restlessness live
in me. I am always
leaving Hungary,
never understanding
the language. I have
been fucking almost
as long as you've been
dead. Every time
it's a miracle even
when it's terrible to dial
into another's skin to call
their name. So many
people live here,
in my skin,
it's getting crowded.
Say my name say
my name say my name—
ask your landlord
to cut me a key.

Rob thinks this poem
is about white guilt.
Ben thinks it's me

coming out. Yes, maybe,
but this poem
is about something
else to me. I thought
if I left Wohler Street,
if I made poems,
if I dated the bass
player and married
the Lord, kept friends
and carried beer
for a living, I'd feel
differently, but I don't.
I don't feel any different.

Mosquitoes lifted
my grandmother
like she was an apron
filled with blackberries
and carried her
into the sky. She hoped
the feeling she called
God would call her
name and she would live
with him, faithful husband
who fixed the crooked
shed door, fed the chickens
and footed his half
of the rent forever
and ever amen.

ACKNOWLEDGEMENTS

Poems from this collection have previously appeared in *Minola Review, Poetry Is Dead, The Rusty Toque, The Puritan, The Walrus, Rattle, PRISM International, Room, The Malahat Review, Plenitude Magazine, Maisonneuve, Arc Poetry Magazine, This Magazine, Forklift, Ohio, Eighteen Bridges, EVENT, The Fiddlehead, Lemon Hound, Bad Nudes,* and *CNQ.* Thank you to all of the editors who gave my poems homes.

"Drunk River" was longlisted for the 2018 CBC poetry prize.

"Girl Like" was a finalist for *Rattle* magazine's 2017 poetry contest.

"Harvest Moon Lantern Festival" won *Arc Poetry Magazine*'s 2017 Poem of the Year Award.

"Vortex Fluid Device" was a finalist for the *Walrus's* 2016 poetry contest.

Funding from the British Columbia Arts Council and the Canada Council for the Arts made this book possible, and I am very grateful for the support.

Thank you to the Storm Crow Tavern and Alehouse in Vancouver, B.C., and in particular to Sean Cranbury and Sydney Gregoire, who kept me employed during the writing of this book. Your flexibility and support kept me alive.

Thank you to Suzannah Showler—this manuscript would probably still be in a drawer without you.

Thank you to Elizabeth Bachinsky and Rhea Tregebov, my eternal and eternally generous mentors.

Thank you to everyone at House of Anansi for taking a chance on this weirdo little book and making it beautiful. In particular, Kevin Connolly, you are the keenest editor and have made this collection so much better; and Alysia Shewchuk, thank you for designing me the hot pink book I've always dreamed of.

So many of my friends appear in these pages and/or have helped edit them. I would like to thank Michelle Brown, Zaq Haslam, Matthew Walsh, Megan Jones, Kyla Jamieson, Shaun Robinson, Christopher Evans, Adèle Barclay, Katrina Sellinger, Jane Campbell, Nadine Bachan, Sierra Skye Gemma, Bardia Sinaee, Claire Matthews, Rob Taylor, Michael Prior, Josiah Neufeld, Aaron Kozak, and especially Angela Prpic. This book is yours.

KAYLA CZAGA is the author of one previous collection of poems, *For Your Safety Please Hold On* (Nightwood Editions, 2014), and the chapbook *Enemy of the People* (Anstruther Press, 2015). Her work has been awarded the Gerald Lampert Memorial Award and the Canadian Authors Association's Emerging Writer Award and has been nominated for the Governor General's Literary Award, the Dorothy Livesay Poetry Prize, and the Debut-litzer. She lives in Victoria, B.C.